ROKC

Leadership
built on the Return on Key
Component

by Alessandro Daliana

About the author

For over two decades, Alessandro Daliana has occupied leadership positions in international companies, and advised investors, boards of directors and executives on how to maximize shareholder value and stakeholder satisfaction through leadership. From this work and independent studies, Alessandro has developed the ROKC method, bringing value to companies across multiple industries.

Alessandro studied at I.M.D. in Lausanne, Switzerland, holds an M.B.A. from Pace University's Lubin School of Business, New York, and a B.A. from Bennington College, Vermont. He lives in New York City.

ROKC
Leadership
built on the Return on Key Component
by Alessandro Daliana

Published by Chokti Inc., New York City, NY

Copyright © 2013 Chokti Inc.
First Edition, 2013

ISBN - 10: 1492284920
ISBN - 13: 978-1492284925

Cover image: Manhattan Schist

For business people everywhere

Acknowledgements

I want to thank my college professor Mansour Farhang without whose advice, so many years ago, to state the obvious this book would never have been written.

My deepest thanks and appreciation also go to my friend, Gwendolyn Alston, who over the years patiently listened to me discuss my business ideas, and who has used her literary talents to read, advise on and edit this book through its many iterations.

I also want to acknowledge all the beta readers Gwen rounded up to for the first renditions of this book. Without their comments and observations, many much-needed improvements would have never happened.

Many thanks also to my family and friends who supported me during this endeavor.

"… everyone who hears these words of mine and puts them into practice is like a wise man who built his house on the rock."

- Matthew 7:24-17

Table of Contents

Leadership built on the ROKC

Introduction

One night while at dinner with a client, we overheard two men at the next table engage in a very passionate discussion about God. This must have been very important subject for them because they talked about God for most of the meal. At one point, their exchange became so impassioned that my client said, "I wish our customers were as passionate about our products as these two are about God." I thought this an odd comment and, brushing it off, continued our conversation. Many months later, that evening came back to me and it set off an "ah ha" moment. Religion is truly the world's oldest business.

Don't take me wrong, I mean no disrespect. All I am doing is drawing an analogy. In my view, religion has the same characteristics as any successful business.

All the successful businesses I know of are built around one asset that provides them with a competitive advantage in their market. In the case of religion, this is often a "God," or many Gods. Everything the business does leverages this asset to provide customers with goods and services that bring them some benefit or another. As the business grows other businesses develop around it.

In the context of religion, God has led to the creation of any number of businesses in areas as disparate as: real estate, publishing, education, music, merchandising, tourism, war, persecution, torture and so on.

From a business standpoint, "God" is similar to a brand because God has no physical manifestation. As such, God must be experienced. Even when God may be the same God for two or more groups of people, God is differentiated. Each group will experience their God differently. Think of the similarities and differences between Catholics and Protestants, Sunnis and Shiites, the three schools of Buddhism (Theravada, Mahāyāna, and Vajrayāna) as well as many other subdivisions, sects and belief systems. The same but different.

Most importantly, the experience of God creates community. Like any successful and robust brand God brings people together. People commune around their God.

Also of note is that, after so many centuries, the capital investment in the brand, God, is really quite small in comparison with the stream of revenues generated by all the businesses that revolve around the God "brand." One might even say the return on investment is unquantifiable and unknowable.

This asset that provides the competitive advantage and around which the business activities revolve is what I refer to as the "key component." The term comes from engineering and refers to the component in a piece of machinery that makes everything else work.

I discovered the key component when I worked for Thomson Multimedia, a consumer electronics company. I was conducting an audit of an audio business where I learned that most of the components used in the CD player were sourced from vendors around the world because they were considered commodities. All the components, that is, except for the optical pickup. The company manufactured the optical pickup because it was the key component. The optical pickup is the device that captures the digital data stored on the CD so that this data can be processed and converted into music for your listening pleasure. In other words, without the optical pickup a CD player wouldn't work.

This component can also be used in other disk driven devices like the DVD player, BluRay player, gaming consoles and any other device that uses a disc medium to store and retrieve data; its community, if you will. Given all these different applications, it made sense to Thomson to build a factory to manufacture the optical pickup. The factory would be able to produce over many years and the profit generated would provide a nice return on the key component, or "ROKC."

For many years, I have used the idea of the key component whenever approaching a business because it is the "key" to the value-creating process. By giving the business its competitive advantage, the key component underpins and drives the business's strategy and organization. Everything needs to come back to the key component. Therefore, all leadership decisions must focus on the key component to maximize shareholder returns and stakeholder satisfaction.

ROKC provides leadership with a methodology they can turn to time and again to keep everyone's activity in focus. Reference to the ROKC reminds all stakeholders of why their business exists and why it does what it does.

The ROKC approach differs significantly from other techniques in its ability to consider the company in its entirety instead of just one facet at a time.

In today's increasingly specialized world, there are a many management techniques vying for a company's dollars, and more being packaged and put on the market every day. These techniques are probably very effective when applied one part of the business. However, leaders need to decide which to apply by taking the business as a whole or be perceived as delegating to others responsibility for decisions that they themselves should be making.

As John Edward Huth wrote in his *New York Times* Opinion piece, dated July 20, 2013, entitled "Losing Our Way in the World":

"Too often in the modern era, we rely on guardians to interpret events for us, and they're too happy to step in and tell us what something 'means'. But when we do this, we surrender the more primal empiricism that our ancestors surely possessed."

Although Mr Huth is talking about life's path, I find that this observation is equally applicable to business. Too often, business people allow technicians--what I call people with a technical knowledge--to tell them the "meaning" of events affecting their business. Worse, these technicians are brought in to define events that affect the business. Even if what these technicians describe may ring true, it lacks our own "primal empiricism," our own conceptual framework.

In viewing the business as a whole, the ROKC method allows decision makers to pick and choose only those management techniques that will maximize the ROKC. Also, using the ROKC method helps the decision maker to better argue their choice as it forces them to examine underlying assumptions, as well as sharing understanding of the business with and increasing the involvement of their fellow decision makers.

In this book, you will discover how to identify the business's key component and put it at the center of your strategy and organization. To help you better understand the ROKC methodology, I break it down into its two major components: the transformative process and risk management. The transformative process defines what the business does to convert the key component into a product the market wants to consume. Everything else is relegated to risk management. In the last section, I explain how to incorporate the ROKC method into your business, using the business planning process as a starting point.

As anyone who knows me will say, I can be verbose and complex so I have made an effort to keep this book short and to use simple language (except where a more technical term adds clarity). I hope I have achieved this goal and that you find the ROKC method as profitable as I do.

- Alessandro Daliana

Leadership built on the ROKC

What is a Business?

Before beginning discussion about the ROKC method, I think it is best to define a business. I know this may appear silly for some readers but in my experience it is important we speak the same language. We don't want to be like the three blind men touching different parts of the same elephant and coming up with disparate views. Each man describes the elephant based on their individual experience--as a wall, a snake, or a tree--and thus they disagree about everything. In other words, they each perceive part of the reality but none comprehends the whole. In the same way, often people attribute a different meaning to the same word, so it is best that we be on the same page from the get go.

By way of illustration, I'll begin with another parable. Once upon a time, two wealthy landowners were in their club drinking a fine cognac and smoking expensive cigars, reminiscing about their lives and how they acquired their wealth. At one point, a disagreement arose over the "common" man's ability to achieve their rank of privilege and wealth. Since neither of them considered himself a "common" man, the dispute was very brief and theoretical. They decided to put their divergent views to the test. They would give one of their workers a parcel of land with a beautiful pine forest on it and see how he managed this new found wealth.

One gentleman was convinced the worker was not very smart and would cut down the trees for a quick profit. He would live large for a while before returning to the company begging them for his old job back. The other thought the worker would be clever and might actually make something of himself.

Much to the first man's surprise, he lost the argument.

The worker did not cut down the trees. Instead, he and his family harvested the pine nuts and sold them at the local market for a profit that they then reinvested. This new landowner understood he could better provide for himself and his family over the long-term by living off of the "fruits" of the trees rather than from the trees themselves. Thus, the worker became an entrepreneur.

Of course, this turn of events in an individual's life is rarely this easy but for our purposes let's say it is so. I like this story because it serves to illustrate a set of attributes I find are common to all businesses:

1. There is an asset that can be put to a productive use (in this case, the pine trees).

2. Work can be employed to turn the asset into a product (harvesting, shelling and selling the nuts).
3. The product (pine nuts) has a perceived benefit/value in the market (consumer buys them), and
4. The market wants to repeatedly consume the product (customers like to regularly eat pine nuts).

Expressed more simply, we could write:

a productive asset + work = product

a product + perceived benefit/value = consumption

As you can see, I state this economic relationship as two equations because having a productive asset that can be transformed into a product is not enough for it to be consumed by the market. The product must also have some perceivable benefit or value for the customer so that they will actually acquire it.

Too often, we come up with business ideas only from the productive side of the equation without giving much thought to the consumption side. This attitude can set us up for failure.

Having productive assets and using them to create a product, even a product customers want, should be the easy part of the business. As we will see, managing the assumptions and risks inherent in the business are the challenge.

Our pine nut entrepreneur may not realize it, but he is making a number of assumptions, some significant and others minor. For example:

- In deciding not to cut down the trees and sell the wood he is assuming the market for pine nuts is better than the one for wood.
- Some plants have a useful productive life so he is assuming the trees will continue to produce pine nuts well into the future.
- Similarly, he is assuming the market will continue to demand pine nuts over a period matching production.
- Likewise, he is assuming he can successfully manage the future challenges his little enterprise will face.

And so on and so forth - the list of assumptions can be very long. What we can say, in a nutshell, is that over the life of the business, the pine nut farmer will be faced with and have to manage many risks.

What was at first a fairly simple expression that focused on making and selling, is rapidly becoming more complex as the notion of risk becomes central to our entrepreneur's business. In fact, managing risk is central to all businesses.

For argument's sake, let's say the pine forest is in a region where people eat pasta with pesto at breakfast, lunch and dinner. Pesto is made with basil leaves, garlic and olive oil and, most importantly, pine nuts. In this market, the entrepreneur will have no trouble selling his production because demand is so high and constant. In other words, the risk of consumption is very low. Consequently, the entrepreneur's primary risk will be to produce enough pine nuts to satisfy demand.

So our wily entrepreneur decides to manage his risk of ensuring the next year's sales by stockpiling part of this year's production. However, when the new year comes around he discovers the pine nuts have become rancid and his clients don't want them. It looks like stocking up pine nuts is not such a good way of managing risk. Lucky for him and those who depend on his enterprise the harvest is good in the second year and he can satisfy demand.

That year he decides to try something new by making pine nut preserve, or jam, for the coming year.

We will give him an "A" for effort but the third year out his clients aren't crazy about this new product because they can't use it in their pesto, it is too sweet. The customers don't buy it. Once again he is a lucky fellow, the spirits of the forest have graced him with a good harvest and allowed him to satisfy everyone.

In preparation for the fourth year, the entrepreneur decides to use fertilizer, hire botanists and caretakers, and employ a variety of goods and services to ensure his production. This approach produces excellent results. His forest produces so much that he can satisfy market demand and has enough left over to compensate everyone who helped make this possible by paying them in pine nuts.

But wait! Some people already have plenty of pine nuts and don't want more. They want to be compensated in other ways: one wants a chicken, another a pig, another an apple pie and so on until the last vendor who wants the farmer's daughter (in marriage, of course).

In agrarian societies, barter systems where everything the community needs is produced and consumed within the community are the norm. But as goods and services come from outside the community other forms of compensation become necessary. As economies evolve and production is more specialized, compensation needs to be portable so money, legal tender, is introduced. No matter where a person is the money in their pocket will be recognized as having the same value in one place as it had when it was acquired in another place.

In the world of money, our entrepreneur sells his pine nuts for units of value that he can use to pay for the goods and services he acquired to take care of his trees. The sellers of those goods and services will in turn use those units of value to acquire their own goods and services, and so on and so forth throughout the economy.

The challenge of the money-based system is bringing the buyer and seller, the parties, to an agreement on the value of the goods and services exchanged, the transaction. In other words, a transactional value must be determined that satisfies both parties. The buyer may consider the seller is overvaluing his product while the seller thinks the buyer is not recognizing the value in his product. Without going into the economics of supply and demand what is in reality at the root of this issue is once again the notion of "risk."

As we saw with our pine nut entrepreneur it took him four years of experimenting before he came up with the best solution to manage the risks inherent in the production side of his business. Remember, we kept consumption constant in this example, in order to focus on production; otherwise, he would have had to manage consumption risk too. The seller, who wants to be in business for many years to come, needs a value that will allow him to experiment. On the other side, the buyer probably wants to use the product immediately so he is bargaining that the product will do what it says it will do:

be useful to make pesto. Now we see that a simple transaction involves a number of unspoken assumptions such as: the short-term and long-term objectives of the parties. The producer has short-term risks associated with making the product and long-term risks because he wants to be in business for a number of years. The buyer mostly has short-term risks related to using the product but also has some longer term risks if he hopes to reacquire the product in the future. So we also have to add that there is a certain level of trust they place in each other that each party will live up to their respective long-term side of the deal. We now need to adjust our once simple expression to consider the parties' short-term and long-term needs and trust in each other.

Hmmm? Trust? How can we give a tangible expression to something that really isn't tangible? The closest I have come to defining this experience is through the concept of "certainty" or, even better, a "reduction of uncertainty." Every successful transactional relationship I know of gives each party a sense that they have somehow reduced uncertainty in their lives. This means that each party puts a degree of trust in the relationship that will involve meeting their respective expectations about the transaction.

The seller expects to create a product that will be in demand and can be sold over the long term. The consumer wishes to purchase a product that will meet their immediate needs or desires, and, depending on the product, do so on a regular basis. If the product meets the consumer's requirements and expectations, they may be willing to pay a value for it that allows the seller to ensure that they have covered (managed) the risks involved in its production and still have something left over to invest for the future.

From this perspective, it becomes clear that the difference in these two risk horizons is what we call "profit," that part of the sale price in excess of the cost of doing business. It is this quantum that allows the seller to reinvest in his business thereby assuring its longevity and the business's ability to fulfill its side of the unspoken contract.

What is important to understand here is that the process used to transform a productive asset into a product needs to generate enough value to pay for all the risk management activities the business must undertake, while leaving a residual amount for reinvestment.

A business can be defined as an economic activity that has a productive asset which can be transformed through work into a product; the product has a perceivable benefit/value identified by the customer who consumes it; the transactional value allows each party to manage their short-term and long-term risks thereby reducing uncertainty.

Leadership built on the ROKC

The Key Component

All businesses have assets used in their processes. In the case of our pine nut entrepreneur, the assets are, for example: land, the trees, access to water, buckets to carry the pinecones, a furnace to open them, hammers to shell the nuts, bags to package them and a cart to get them to market, amongst others. These assets are specific to the tasks the business needs to accomplish. As important as these assets may be, most are at the service of one primary asset: the key component. In other words, there is one asset that makes all the other assets necessary. The key component is the foundation upon which the business is built.

A key component can be just about anything and for every business it will be different. Often the key component is a thing, a tangible asset, such as a machine. In other cases, it is a non-thing, an intangible asset, such as a brand. In still others, it may be a right to use someone else's asset or an asset built or acquired. Whatever the case, a key component has the distinction of providing a competitive advantage in the market in which it used.

Competitive advantage is key to any successful business because it allows the business to function as a business. By identifying the key component it is easier to discern the competitive advantage because that advantage becomes tangible as it is manifested by an asset, even an intangible asset. The key component becomes the point of focus for the business. A business that is unable to identify its competitive advantage will not distinguish itself from a competitor making it a "me-too" business. This is why it is important to evaluate the competitive advantage the key component provides within the market the business operates.

Let's take a pizza restaurant as an example. A person coming to a town that has no pizzerias for miles around may find a fertile market for pizza. This person's knowledge of pizza-making is their key component and, without competition, he may use this knowledge to build a successful business. Since there is no direct competition, the pizza maker can even make a "not so good" product but people will still flock to his store. The day another pizza store opens in town, the customers will have something to compare with and may stop patronizing the first store because their product is "not so good." The first pizzeria, losing its competitive advantage in pizza-making, will have to find a new one. The owners may decide to try to get their clients back by making some other product like pasta to serve in their store or determine that what really mattered was the dough so they make breads and sell the dough to customers who make pizza at home or find that their tomato sauce is particularly good and sell it to the people in town and export it to the next town over.

Thus, changes in the competitive landscape over the life of a business may result in changes in the key component. How and when these changes are perceived by the business's leaders often means the difference between the life and death of the business, making the management of risks to the competitive advantage of a key component the number one priority for any business.

A good example of such evolutionary changes is the luxury goods company LVMH. Most probably, Louis Vuitton, the "LV" in "LVMH," started out as an artisanal manufacturer of quality leather products where the key component was his craftsmanship. The sale of leather goods must have generated enough profit to allow him to hire and train apprentices to work in his booming business. At that stage, the key component became education. Later on, with industrialization, that know-how was passed along to engineers who built machines to automate parts of the process, our secondary assets, so then the engineers might be considered the key component. More recently, the key component became the brand: Louis Vuitton. The company puts its brand on its own leather goods as well as on accessories, clothing, yacht racing, hotels, and so on, so its consumers can associate the brand with the luxury experience provided by these goods and services.

What is noteworthy is how the relative cost of the key component reduces over time with respect to the number of products and services to which it is applied. It is not hard to imagine that the expenditure for Mr. Vuitton to learn his skills and develop his business was higher than that of teaching his apprentices, which was in turn higher than getting the machines to do part of the work, which was then more costly than licensing the brand to companies whose goods and services benefit from it. This suggests that relative cost is also a fundamental criteria for identifying the key component.

In financial terms, the key component must have a cost that is relatively low as compared with the future stream of revenues brought by the sale of the products or services produced. In other words, the initial investment in the key component will be paid back quickly so that the return on the key component can be maximized over as long a period as possible. Understood within the context of potential changes in the key component, the horizon may be long or short but in every case uncertain.

The founders of Google may have started out with an algorithm that improved search results but the initial investment received an ample return through the advertising model that was developed. Think of how many ad impressions are made per day, all based on that algorithm. The algorithm is literally "sold" millions of times per day.

Examples of key components are:

- LVMH, a luxury goods company, the brand portfolio.
- Google, its search algorithm.

And:

- A lawyer, their knowledge; a combination of education and experience.
- Facebook, user engagement.
- An airline, customer service.

It is the centrality of the key component to a business that the makes it the best way of managing a business: the Return on Key Component, the ROKC.

The key component is the asset that:

- provides the business with a competitive advantage in the market it serves,
- changes in the perceived competitive advantage may oblige the company to change key components,
- the key component has a value that is relatively low as compared with the future stream of benefits it can generate, which
- maximizes shareholder value.

Worksheet

What is your business's key component?

What is the competitive advantage the key component provides your business in the market(s) within which it operates?

The Transformative Process

In developing the ROKC method, I found its application easier to understand by separating the business into its component parts:

- the key component,
- the transformative process whereby the key component is made into a salable product, and
- the risk management activities the business engages with respect to the first two.

Admittedly, this distinction can sometimes appear arbitrary because everything is so interconnected. Nonetheless, it is a practical way of understanding, managing a business.

In much the same way we identify and isolate the key component from all the other assets in the business, here we will identify and isolate the business the process by which the business uses the key component to create a product from risk management activities. By focusing on the transformative process distinctly from risk management we are able to view the business in its simplest form.

The transformative process can then split into its two parts:

- the process of producing the product and
- the process by which the product is consumed.

Interestingly, by understanding the business by looking at these three elements, it becomes clear that the level of value-added at this point must be high enough to enable the business to satisfy all its risk management needs, financing obligations and still provide a profit that can be reinvested in the business. In other words, if by considering only these three elements the business does not produce a significant value-added then the business is probably not viable.

The Productive Process

The "Productive Process" is the process by which the business uses the key component to create the product(s) the customer *may* want to consume. This process involves work.

Work comes in two forms: manual and automated. In the case of manual labor, work involves an individual using a tool of some sort (hammer, saw, truck, computer, pen) and in the automated case, there is a machine that supplies the labor. The typical example of automated labor is a machine that makes widgets. A more recent example is a computer program that automates the process by which data is turned into information.

Using an example, Google's founders worked very hard to create the search engine which is made up of two distinct parts: the search algorithm and the bots that collect the data. The former is the key component because without it the information the bots accumulated would be useless thus the latter is part of the productive process to make something useful from the key component. In this example, the transformative process involves the work that goes into writing the code for the bots as well as that required for the storage and management of the data in the database.

In the productive process, we are interested in all the different inputs a business needs to make a product that can be proposed to the market. Transforming a key component into a marketable product may require a course of study, an apprenticeship, setting up a production facility, an office, a store, a vehicle, computer programming knowledge, fuel, chemicals, components, and so on. Likewise, this process needs people who can apply their own dose of labor in the use of these inputs and others to plan and manage the processes.

There is no fully automated transformative process known to man except those that exist in nature making the human labor component of the productive process equally, if not more, important than the automated part. All tools need have a well trained and knowledgable user manipulating them. Finding the right human resources to employ in the productive process can be challenging so we hold off on this discussion until later in the book. We have dedicated a whole section to talent and management risk.

When looking at the work involved in transforming a key component into a product the market may want the value creation part of the equation can be challenging. This is where the business leader must exercise their craft by achieving the proper balance between value and safety. A company may decide to file a patent to protect an invention, its key component, which means a certain amount of work will be needed for administering the back and forth with the patent office and the lawyer. Another company may file five patents all at once because they want to be extra sure they are protecting their invention, without really considering that this will mean five times the administrative work. Assuming one patent was enough, those extra hours of work take away from other activities. This is not a very efficient allocation of resources.

In order to maximize the return on the key component leadership must make the right decisions about resource allocation. Below is a brief story to illustrate how resource allocation in the productive process might be best viewed.

Imagine, if you will, being shipwrecked on a desert island. You are alone, wet, tired, thirsty, and hungry. You set off to explore your new surroundings when you discover there are plenty of rabbits inhabiting the island. You grab the first branch you find and take off in search of the next meal. You spot a rabbit and try to sneak up on it, but it hears you and runs away. Off you go, running after it. After some time chasing the rabbit, you get tired and it gets away. Having expended a lot of precious energy, you are now even hungrier than before. Not wanting to be bested by a rabbit, you give chase a few more times before finally giving up.

While you are regaining your strength, you remember a TV episode of Bear Grylls, in which he uses snares to trap small animals. You decide to give it a try. You fashion a few traps and set them up at the entrance of what you hope are rabbit dens. The next day, still hungry but excited with anticipation of a good meal, you set off to see the results of your efforts. To your surprise, the snare worked, you caught a rabbit. Victory is yours! Now, if you could only remember how Bear cleans the rabbit and makes a fire!

What is the lesson from this story? Running after and clubbing small prey causes you to burn a lot of calories which is less efficient than the more sedentary activity of trapping them. Our ancestors understood this since it meant the difference between life and death. Never use more calories getting your food than the calories you will be consuming.

The same is true in business. Having a key component that can be turned into a product is only the beginning. The process to convert it into a product must employ less value than the value the company will gain from its sale. This means the productive process must be simple and easy. The simpler and easier the productive process is the more reproducible the results, the lower the uncertainty of the outcome, and the higher the ROKC. As a result of the productive process we want the ROKC to be very high so that all the other activities and obligations the business has to face can be dealt with. We'll see more about this in the upcoming chapters.

The process by which a key component is transformed into a product must employ fewer resources and less value than those the company will gain from its sale thereby maximizing ROKC.

The Consumption Process

Having a key component and a way to efficiently and economically convert it into a product does not mean that the market will perceive the benefit or value of it and consume it. A producer must create their product in such a way as to communicate and persuade the buyer of its benefit and value. The best way to bridge this perception gap is to present the product as a way for *buyers* to get their own return on their own key component.

Consumer products companies are particularly good at this. They present their customers with products the customer perceives will enhance their natural features. Products to be healthier, more attractive, more dynamic, richer, happier, sexier, and so on. While business-oriented companies position their products to enhance their client's own transformative processes by increasing productivity, competitiveness, and profitability.

Since no producer is able to guarantee these benefits, the product is presented with the promise to *reduce the uncertainty* of not having the enhancements it offers.

If we continue with the Google example above, having a winning search algorithm, bots and database is not enough to make the system useful. The company had to develop a user interface allowing for terms to be submitted and search results to be displayed in such a way that made sense. The text box for submitting search terms is fairly straightforward but the search results page is constantly evolving, even now, after so many years. Both of these activities allow the user to win but not the company. Consequently, engineers built the advertising system into the search process. Advertisers pay for their URL to appear in the search results thus creating a win also for Google.

Again, there is human component that needs to be included here. The business must employ the best and the brightest to help it efficient translate what it creates into a product with meaning for the consumer. These people must understand the market well enough to create a community of users who will not only consume the product once but do so continuously and act as standard bearers, or ambassadors, for it.

The first challenge a business faces is defining the target market. An investor once showed me a business plan for a gelateria, an Italian ice cream store, based on national market figures instead of the half-mile to a mile radius around the chosen location. Did he really think he was going to sell to the whole country from one store? No. He first had to capture the attention and the palates of the market closest to his product. The hard part of the target market process is to define within a geographic area who in that population might be interested in the product, and for whom there may be a potential win-win. Are there families with young children in the area? Surely, they would be good customers. Maybe the store is located on a particularly well traveled street with lots of foot traffic? Also, a good source of customers. A quiet street corner in a rural area is probably not a good place for a gelateria.

The second challenge is determining the features and characteristics of interest to those potential customers. The base product might be vanilla which can be improved upon by adding toppings: chocolate chips, chocolate syrup, cherries or nuts. Or, the product offer can be expanded to include other flavors: chocolate, strawberry or bacon. Other bases can be added like custard or yogurt. Tailoring the product to the market is important.

Having understood who is the target customer and what they want, the business must let them know that they are there to serve them. Communicating with the customer can be a tricky process because, in my view, there is an inverse relationship between the distribution and communication. The more widely available a product is, the less communication the company needs to do and vice-versa. The gelateria is one store, operating in a market made up of roughly a one-mile radius, thus the bulk of their clientele will be made up of passerby. Efforts to increase their market might involve communicating outside the one-mile radius. Whereas, doing these activities within the one-mile radius would probably be a waste of resources.

A more pointed example of this inverse relationship can be found in e-commerce. Technically speaking a product sold online is available everywhere so communication would be limited but this is not the case. Although the product is available everywhere the e-commerce site is not making it more difficult to find than a corner store As a result, e-commerce sites employ a significant amount of company resources on communication, so much so that the term "cost of acquiring a client" is synonymous with online business.

This brings us to the last challenge which is relative value, or more simply, price. The seller wants to get enough from the buyer to cover the transformative process while creating enough of an excess to mitigate its risks and reinvest for the future. The buyer, who is probably be using the product in the near future, may not want to recognize that excess value that the seller may need because there are many competitors and substitutes available in the market. A careful balance needs to be established. In the case of the gelateria, the business will have direct competitors, other ice cream stores, and indirect ones, substitutes for ice cream, all competing for the same customers. Knowing the competition's pricing limits may be a determining factor in the business's success and failure.

These challenges are known as the "4Ps": product, place, promotion, and price. They are the very basics of marketing which makes them important concepts to master.

But all the Ps in the world don't matter if the win-win/ reduction in uncertainty attribute is not achieved. Our gelateria may do everything right and still not succeed. A very good example of a company that was able to succeed where everyone else failed is Apple with the launch of the iPod.

At the turn of the century - that's the 21st century - there were many mp3 players on the market but none were successful. Using these players required ripping a CD onto the user's computer hard drive, then transferring it into a file management system and synching the library with the player. Like the first computers, this activity was mainly the realm of people with lots of technical knowledge, enough to feel comfortable with go through a process that used different software packages. Then, Apple introduced the iPod and everything changed.

The iPod reduced the uncertainty of going from library to device. With the click of a button a user could seamlessly move music files from the iTunes store to their iTunes software and onto their iPod. Even ripped CDs could be managed through the iTunes software allowing the user to add their existing music collection to the music bought online.

No doubt Apple's technical knowledge was useful in building the iPod and the iTunes store and file management software but the company didn't have any content. The music industry had just taken a hit from file sharing services, like Napster, that allowed users to exchange files free of charge, and was looking for a way to remain relevant in the future. Apple offered the industry a solution that no one else could, so they signed up. Without these music licensing agreements and the digital rights management software needed to manage them, Apple would have probably met with limited success.

So, it is important to understand that Apple entered a market that already existed and was large enough to be worthwhile entering. Apple obtained a big chunk of the music industry's sales. The iPod/iTunes system provided a win-win solution for the music companies, the music consumers, and Apple.

Create a win-win situation that reduces uncertainty for both the buyer and the seller, and maximizes the ROKC.

Worksheet

Describe the process by which the business transforms the key component into a product.

How do customers perceive the benefits and value of the product?

How does the business create a win-win situation with its customers?

Leadership built on the ROKC

The Business Model & Mission Statement

Taken together, the key component and the transformative process are the business model: a simple expression of how the business creates value. This value creation process must be sufficiently robust and significant to allow the business to manage risks and remain in existence over time.

The business model is succinctly expressed in the mission statement: one or two simple sentences that describe what the business does. By design, it is market focused so that all stakeholders can readily understand it.

Whittling the statement down to one or sentences can be very challenging. The more complex a business is, the harder it is to elaborate a simple statement. We don't want a run-on sentence dignified of Proust; we want something simple. However, not too simple or the statement may not succeed in differentiating the business from the competition.

One of the companies I worked for, Geopost, went through a period of rapid growth by acquisition which resulted in an identity problem. During the process of integrating all the new companies, top management decided the holding company needed to rework its mission statement. I will never forget how much time and money went into this process. Meetings with around 20 senior executives lasting hours at a time, other meetings held with around 50 executives for more hours, and then different consultants brought in to accompany the process. All this cost millions in time and money. It was no small affair.

The question was: Is Geopost in the parcel transportation or logistics business? In very simple terms, a transport company moves goods from point A to point B and a logistics company provides a much higher value added service to clients, providing them with a supply chain solution. Regardless of the definition we eventually agreed on, it had to conform with our means of production and company know-how.

Having a robust mission statement is not an easy task. It requires a good understanding of what business the company is in. The process of defining the mission statement can be lengthy and costly but should pay off in the future through effective communication with stakeholders. It is worthwhile to take the time necessary to write up a solid statement.

A mission statement is one or two sentences that explains the business model to stakeholders.

Worksheet

Describe your business model.

Write your company's mission statement.

How much ROKC does the business model create?

Leadership built on the ROKC

Risk Management

Beyond the business model, everything else a business does is risk management. Inherent in any activity are small and large risks that can affect the key component, the productive and the consumption process. Some of these risks will be internal to the company while others will come from outside. Internal risks can be having the right person in the right job or organizing the job so that just about anyone can do it or having the expertise to make the right decisions or any other internal facet of the company. External risks can come from the competition, changes in legislation, acts of God, or any other factors affecting the business environment.

In the ROKC method, we seek to make a clear distinction between the business model and risk management because the former is seen as needing to produce value-added high enough to cover the value destruction of the latter. For the most part, risk management is assumed to be a cost that reduces the ROKC. Only really exceptional risk management can add value, which is fairly rare.

The recommended method for examining risks is the SWOT analysis. It has been around for years and works but you can use any method you are most comfortable with. The approach is fairly straightforward: the "SW" stands for

"Strengths" and "Weaknesses" and the "OT" for "Opportunities" and "Threats." Although these terms may appear to have the same meaning they are in fact very distinct. The "SW" refers to what is *inside* the company and "OT" to what is *outside* of the company.

For our purposes a "risk" is neutral. It is the viewer perspective within a given context that makes it a positive or a negative. Let me explain.

Many of you may have been to a job interview during which the interviewer asks you what are your strengths and weaknesses. This usually leaves the interviewee, you, feeling frustrated and dumbfounded because a strength might be a weakness in the potential employers business's environment. In fact, how your answer is interpreted by the interviewer is conditioned by their knowledge of the company's values and culture. Which can only be an assumption for you since you have no direct experience of the company. The lack of a shared perspective skews such a question in favor of the employer so answering it may end up working against you and you are there to get the job.

It is important to first understand the assumptions that underpin the question. In the case of the job interview question, it is best to stop and ask the interviewer to provide you will some background before answering. This helps build a shares set of assumptions on which to build your answer.

Explicitly stating assumptions is fundamental for effective communication and understanding. On the one hand, we develop an awareness of our own set of assumptions which helps us learn more about ourselves. On the other, it helps the listener/reader learn about the speaker/writer thus strengthen the bond between them. Lastly, sharing assumptions also allows others to participate in and share responsibility for the decision-making process.

When working for London International Group, the then owners of Durex condoms, we brought in the consultancy, McKinsey, to work with us on a strategic business review. After conducting a round of interviews with key executives and managers, the McKinsey team organized a meeting where there was a single topic of conversation: assumptions. It was only after we had all agreed to the principal assumptions that McKinsey put together the plan. The McKinsey approach is built around assumptions because they know that once these are agreed to, there is little chance of contesting the plan they produce. You have to go back to the assumptions to make major changes. Being explicit about assumptions is fundamental to managing any dynamic situation.

Using the SWOT analysis you should identify many risks affecting the business model, the significance of which will be conditioned by the shared assumptions underpinning them. Since it is not an efficient use of company resources to focus on all of them, leadership should concentrate only on those affecting competitive advantage, thus the ROKC.

Competitive Advantage Risks

The key component provides the business with its competitive edge, thus making it the crown jewel of the business. But, as we saw above, this competitive advantage is not eternal it changes with the competitive landscape. The competitive advantage the key component provides the business today may not be as effective tomorrow.

A business needs to be constantly vigilant for direct and indirect competitors who can reduce its competitive advantage. Competitors can come into the market with a "better mousetrap", reducing competitiveness and taking business away. Above, we presented the optical pickup, a key component that lost its competitive advantage in an Internet-connected device world to Cloud storage services, like Dropbox and Google Drive.

But innovation can be a tricky thing. There are new technologies developed every day that fall short of their potential and remain on shelves for a long, long time. One example is the RFID tag, Radio Frequency Identification, used during World War II to distinguish friendly aircraft from the enemy's. When the patents expired on this technology, RFID tags were trumpeted as a technology that would revolutionize the supply chain by providing efficiency gains in warehousing and transportation. Later, the technology was used to revolutionize electronic payment systems and advertising. Both much-touted revolution that still haven't occurred possibly because the competitive advantage of the RFID tag is not sufficiently large in comparison with competing technologies. For example, the less costly QR code can be programmed on any computer and printed by any printer.

And innovation does not stop there. A new product called Soundpaper, by Labels That Talk Ltd., allows users to add sound to barcodes also using any computer and printed on any printer. Using a smartphone or a dedicated reader anyone can listen to the recorded message. And then there is the amazing Kate Stone who uses an ordinary printer and special ink to print whole electronic devices on paper. If the technology can make the leap from the laboratory to commercial use this may create a huge competitive advantage in applications like money.

Aside from the technological innovations that may occur in a market there are barriers to entry. Like walking into a room and closing the door behind you, companies try to barricade themselves in their market by making it increasingly expensive to dislodge them. The simplest barrier to entry is a product that is so much a part of the market's culture that no one truly questions its use. In the pine nut example above we assumed the consumers in the market ate pesto morning, noon and night, so pine nuts were in constant demand. Even though that was an assumption in the real market that happens all the time. One of my favorite examples is the history of Kellogg's Corn Flakes.

At the end of the 19th century, Dr. Kellogg, a Seven Day Adventist, who treated patients for constipation at Battle Creek Sanitarium in Michigan, and his brother Will Keith Kellogg allowed some wheat to overcook. Being on a tight budget they tried to do something with it by rolling it out like dough and baking it. When it came out of the oven there were flakes and the patients loved them. They continued to experiment with different grains until they came upon corn flakes. In 1906, the Battle Creek Toasted Corn Flake Company was born.

The dietary habits of the day were very poor and disturbed a great number of people. Those wealthy enough sought treatment at Battle Creek, the rest bought boxes of Corn Flakes from their local general store.

Today's average diet is much richer in fiber making the consumption of Corn Flakes, and other cereals, unnecessary. And yet, people around the world continue to eat them because they are perceived to be part of a healthy diet. In fact, some cereal brands position themselves as health products ("Start of healthy day", "Heart Healthy", "Lower Cholesterol",..) thereby remaining relevant to consumers. Three dates have as much fiber as a bowl of cereal but not many people want to eat dates.

Breakfast cereals are not the only consumer product to have this privileged position in the collective consciousness, there are others, all of which are culturally based. In many places, the consumer can buy seasonal fruits and vegetables all year round making their conservation unnecessary. So products like strawberry jam, canned peas, cured hams and any other preserve or conserve are more the result of memories of our past than of immediate needs. They all benefit from that nature barrier to entry which is customs, habits and culture making it possible for these producers to maintain their relative competitive advantage and generate their ROKC.

Other barriers to entry are man-made. Years ago, the big French Champagne producers introduced a regulatory reform requiring that corks be more compressed when inserted into the bottle. The machines to compress the corks were very expensive. As a result, many small producers found themselves obliged to sell their grapes, the key component, to the big companies effectively making them a commodity.

Since the whole business is built around the competitive advantage provided by the key component the latter needs to be treated like the Queen's crown jewels in the Tower of London: visible to all but closely guarded. The first thing we have to do is to protect the key component from any form of harm.

This would be fine except for the fact that we are already making an assumption: ownership of the key component. Securing ownership is first.

Most, if not all, legal systems recognize ownership in one way or another. Some forms of ownership are titles, deeds, patents, trademarks, copyrights, share certificates, and so on. Even though the same term is used to indicate the same form of ownership the actual rights and privileges may vary from jurisdiction to jurisdiction.

A patent is a form of legal protection given by the state bestowing a monopoly over that intellectual property. No one can use it without the owner's consent. And yet, even with governmental recognition patent disputes break out every day. Thus, ownership is an area of risk even when it is recognized by the state.

Assuming ownership over the key component is as secure as it can be, we can return to preservation the key component. Generally, the first form of protection is physical. A building will install a sprinkler system to protect the property against fire. A house by the beach might have a sand bank in front of it to protect from the sea. A computer or server will be protected from water by placing it on a raised floor. People might be protected by wearing special clothes. Next is insurance. An insurance policy will cover most of the material impairment or destruction of an asset, like the key component. Not only should careful attention be given to the risks being covered but to the insurable value, loss limits, new or used value, deductible, and other contractual terms. The last form of preservation is maintenance and upkeep without which none of the benefits derived from the above will matter.

We have limited ourselves to competitive advantage, ownership and preservation because they focus on what we are trying to achieve: maximizing the ROKC. We need to ensure the key component is competitive, that company owns the rights to that competitive advantage and that it is preserved over its useful life time before being replaced by a new key component. Each one of these risk areas needs to be managed with an eye to not reducing the added-value created by the business model by too much because there may be plenty of other areas of risk to manage as we will see below.

Productive Process Risks

Transforming a key component into a marketable product requires a process that involves talented collaborators using tools to facilitate the task. Just like our ancestors chiseled away at a rock to make an arrowhead or a wheel, modern man produces and uses a wide array of tools. Both the tools we use and the skills required to use them bring about a series of risks that we will examine next.

Production Risks

Productive processes employ tools of one kind or another: machines, hand tools, computers, servers, vehicles, what have you. All of which are designed to work within specific parameters. The closer they get to the limits of these parameters, the higher the risk of non-performance before they ultimately fail. Therefore, a business needs to manage the use of their productive assets' capabilities to minimize the risk of the process slowing or breaking down.

A few examples of the parameters within which tools function properly are: temperature and pressure, capacity, access to materials, timeliness, and so on. Even a tool such as an iPhone works within certain performance parameters, like for temperature. On the Apple website there is an article entitled, "iOS devices: Keeping device within acceptable operating temperatures", that applies to iPhone, iPad, and iPod touch (4th generation and later), it states:

"Operate iOS devices where the temperature is between 0° and 35° C (32° to 95° F). Low- or high-temperature conditions might temporarily shorten battery life or cause the device to alter its behavior to regulate its temperature.

Store the device where the temperature is between -20° and 45° C (-4° to 113° F). Don't leave the device in your car, because temperatures in parked cars can exceed this range.

When using the device or charging the battery, it is normal for it to get warm. The exterior of the device functions as a cooling surface that transfers heat from inside the device to the cooler air outside.

Conditions and activities that may cause the device to alter performance and behavior include:

- Leaving the device in a car on a hot day.
- Leaving the device in direct sunlight for an extended period of time.
- Using certain features in hot conditions or direct sunlight for an extended period of time, such as GPS tracking or navigation in a car, or playing a graphics-intensive game.

If the interior temperature of the device exceeds the normal operating range, the device will protect its internal components by attempting to regulate its temperature. If this occurs,..."

Each industry, sector, and product has its own general and specific risks in this area.

In a transportation business, like the business GeoPost that I cited in a previous chapter, the production process involved vehicles to pick up and deliver parcels, trucks to haul the parcels from one hub to the next and smaller trucks to transport the parcels between the hub to the sorting centers. In the hubs and sorting centers the company used great big automated sorting machines. These machines sort parcels by moving them along a conveyor belt where scanners read the barcode and software pilots a system of shuttles to move the parcel in one direction or another until it reaches the belt that takes it into the truck or delivery van. To better imagine the automated sorting system think of your baggage on the airport carrousel, but much bigger. I could go on and on describing all the other tools the business used, right down to the handcarts and staples, but you might get bored.

The main idea is that many tools can be used, all of which are at risk of not working properly, and potentially bringing the productive process to a screeching halt.

Most of these tools are assets, thus subject to the same risks as the key component, which is also an asset. They share the same risks, such as: ownership rights, insurance, preservation, as well as the performance parameters described above.

The risks affecting the productive process are generally manageable for the business even though unforeseen events may lead to breakage and catastrophic failure.

Then, there are the risks that the company has little influence over, the external risks. These risks may include legislation and regulation as we saw for the key component but also economics. Unless the business owns all the inputs used in the process - which is increasingly rare as business becomes more specialized - the price the business pays and the timeliness with which products are delivered may have a significant affect on the business's ability to maximize ROKC.

At GeoPost, the fleet of trucks needed fuel to run, making the management of fuel costs a significant endeavor. In times when fuel prices were very volatile some competitors, like Fedex and UPS, charge customers a fuel surcharge effectively passing that risk on to their customers. GeoPost couldn't do that because it was indirectly owned by the French Government making it politically unappealing to ask the French customer to pay a fuel surcharge. The company had to make up the cost in other ways or take the hit and reduce the ROKC.

Other inputs a business may require might be: mineral ores, chemicals, electricity, subassemblies, components, software and software updates, information, and so on, exposing them to other risks.

The process of production may involve selecting tools that enhance the competitive advantage in a certain market segment but not in another. One graphic designer might be happy with Photoshop Elements while another chooses Photoshop CC, thus allowing the latter to provide customers with services that the former cannot as there are many more features built into the CC version.

Likewise, there may be risks inherent in the process itself, in the way in which a business makes their product. One of my favorite examples of process is drying laundry.

Growing up, I watched my grandmother hang the laundry on a clothesline using clothespins to hold them down. I never questioned why she did this. One day, however, while doing research for a website I launched, I found a video about Mumbai's open air laundry, Dhobi Ghat, that challenged my understanding of the laundry hanging process.

Over generations, the workers of Dhobi Ghat developed a process of drying laundry that uses fewer resources, provides greater productivity and involves fewer risks. Instead of using a single line with clothespins like my grandmother did, they double up the line and twist it. This way each new garment added to the line, by its shear weight, increases the pressure between the two lines thus holding all the garments more firmly in place. They have no need for the added cost of clothes pins and the extra step necessary to use them. This results in workers hanging clothes faster, thus with a higher productivity. Not using clothespins also increases the quality of the service because the garment is never stained by the metal used to make them, which tends to rust. Thus, there is a reduction in the risk of not providing clients with an immaculately clean garment.

The competitiveness of a process is sometimes less about technology and more a question of how we frame the problem. After seeing this process, I had to ask why we didn't do the same? After a closer look, I came to the conclusion that clothespins are necessary because rack manufacturers make their products so that they only allow one line width of cord to pass through the holes. A single strand of clotheslines dictates the use of clothespins.

Once again we are forced to come full circle and face our assumptions. Although assumptions help us develop short cuts to understanding the world they can also blind us to simple solutions like the one found by the workers at Dhobi Ghat.

The process by which a key component is transformed into a product often requires the use of tools and a production process, both of which involve risks. Managing those risks requires not only understanding the assumptions that support that way of doing things but must also be done in a way that maximizes the ROKC.

Supply Chain Risks

Above I only briefly mentioned the timeliness with which inputs arrive at the production site because I wanted to put off this part of the transformative process so it could be treated separately. Supply chain management is very important in post-industrial economies because these economies focus on consumption instead of production.

Nonetheless the processes and risks are the same for both consumption and production, so I wanted to treat them as one subject.

As the more economically developed countries move away from manufacturing and toward consumption the timely supply of goods becomes fundamental to the business's ability to make good on its promise to its clients. Managing the supply chain and its risk requires tools that are informative instead of physical; in other words, software. Supply chain management seeks to manage the risks associated with the physical flow of goods.

In some cases supply chain management can be simple. A company working with a manufacturer in Asia will probably track its finished products from the plant through their third party logistics partner who does everything from picking up the palettes at the factory gate to shipping the individual items to the final customer. They will do all the intermediate steps such as: order management, export documentation, loading the containers on a ship, customs clearance, shipping to a warehouse, unpacking/stocking, picking and packing, and shipping to the final customer.

On the other hand, supply chain management can be as complex as managing the sourcing of raw material, or components, in one country then shipping them to another where they are converted into semi-finished product before moving on to a third country for assembly into a finished product and being shipping to a retail outlet or final client. Here, too, all the individual steps in between have to be done, but this time it may be a mix of third parties and in-house resources in any possible combination making the sharing of information an even more significant factor for success than the simple version above.

Having the appropriate information management system for the needs of the business and the people who know how to use them are key risk management tools used to maximize the ROKC.

The processes described up to now put the emphasis on the business's internal resources, or the Strengths and Weaknesses, but there are also Opportunities and Threats, factors outside the business's influence. These external factors may be weather, civil actions/war, labor movements/strikes, damage during transportation, piracy or any other event that can affect the physical movement of products. Some can be managed and others not. Each risk needs to be examined individually and the correct course of action determined. A business's ability to manage the risks associated with the physical flow of goods may have a significant affect on the ROKC.

Project Management Risks

Closely associated with Supply Chain Management is Project Management.

In the world of networked businesses, it is inevitable that people in different locations be asked to work together. Like virtual companies, these groups of people come together for a time to complete a particular task before splitting apart and coming together in another combination later on. It falls to the project manager to coordinate these individuals using the best information technology tools available. These increasingly sophisticated systems help the project manager keep all members informed about the project's advancement. They manage project risk by giving a clear and shared view of the project's planning. They allow users to share documents, post updates, engage in chats. Some allow conference calling and more recently video conferencing among many users.

Some businesses have opted for going outside the box, the computer, by investing in telepresence systems. Companies like Fellow Robots, Cisco/iRobot and double robotics, to name just a few, have devices that allow the user to take control of a remotely located robot, "Skype-on-Wheels," and travel throughout the location to work with others as if they were themselves physically present. The robot becomes their avatar, if you will.

A good example of project management risks might be the case of a pharmaceutical company taking a product from the laboratory to production. There are many processes that work well in a lab but then don't when you try to scale them up for industrial production. Sometimes, constant adjustments and even innovation are necessary. For example, in the case of the pharmaceutical company, the research team is in Zurich (Switzerland), product development in Princeton (New Jersey, USA), manufacturing for the active compound in New Delhi (India), manufacturing for the finished product and packaging in Kuala Lumpur (Malaysia) and, because the product is only authorized for sale by the FDA, marketing and sales are in the U.S. The project manager, located anywhere in the world, must manage this far-flung group of people in such a way that they can all work together to resolve any challenges they encounter. The people in India will have to coordinate with those in Switzerland while they scale up production. Whatever modifications the Indians make to the product have to be coordinated with the people in New Jersey who don't want to delay fulfilling customer orders because of an amendment to their FDA authorization. Meanwhile, the people in Malaysia are getting antsy because every delay in receiving the active compound means less time for them to manufacture the finished product needed to fill the U.S. orders. Any change in timing has repercussions down the line. So all this orchestration needs to be done within budget or risk having it fall short of the ROKC target set by management; which in turn may ruin the CEO's credibility with the board, shareholders, and analysts, thereby moving the share price down and reducing everyone's net worth along with it.

To avoid such disasters, the company will monitor the project manager's performance with a Quality Control team using cutting edge statistical methods to measure everything and make corrective recommendations for anything they see as going awry based on benchmarks and knowledge obtained by monitoring other projects.

At an even simpler level, anyone who has tried to have a website built offshore might be familiar with some of the challenges described above. In many cases, the website is delivered months after the agreed delivery date because the service provider is too small to have a very sophisticated project management system. Probably, even if they did have the project management system in place, the employees would not use it because the concept of time is totally different from country to country. Even small projects conducted with small service providers have a variety of risks that need to managed.

In contrast to supply chain management, project management is very assumption-based; the whole project plan is nothing but assumptions until each step is achieved. Don't get me wrong, there are assumptions in supply chain management but in my view they are fairly limited and usually managed through contractual agreements, which is why I didn't bring them up in the previous section. Project Management, on the other hand, is highly steeped in assumptions.

Any step in the project may take longer to complete because one of the assumptions underpinning it was wrong. An experienced project manager knows not to be overly ambitious. Like many business activities, as much as we try to make it a science, it is really an art.

Managing project risk requires a good understanding of the assumptions used during the planning phase to ensure the project comes in on time and within budget to maximize the ROKC.

Consumption Risks

Now that we have examined a number of risk areas specific to the production and supply side of a business, which allow it to potentially push product into a market, we will look at the consumption side of the equation, or the pull side.

To survive, a business cannot limit itself to making a product and hope that someone will want it. The product has to be bought and consumed, and preferably, numerous times over.

A really heart-wrenching example of not only a good product but a great one is that of singer-songwriter Sexto Rodriguez. In the Academy Award-winning documentary "Looking for Sugarman," the filmmaker recounts Mr. Rodriguez's story telling us that his music, comparable to Bob Dylan both in poetry and musical score, remained almost entirely unrecognized in the United States while achieving almost mythic success and status in South Africa. In fact, the U.S. record producer went so far as to state that he didn't think that more than half a dozen records had sold in America when he cancelled his contract with the singer.

As discussed in the transformative process section, this is best achieved by creating a win-win relationship between the business and the customer. It is probably safe to argue that the South African market identified very strongly with the messages communicated in Sexto Rodriguez's songs because of the period in history the country was living; there was a strong bond between the two. In the U.S., this connection was not made.

No matter what the product, getting traction in a market is not an exact science. There are just too many variables to consider, making any go-to-market strategy nothing better than an educated guess. In essence, everything the business thinks about its product and the market are nothing more than assumptions that need to be tested in the real world.

Whatever risk management activities the business engages in they need to create and maintain a connection with the customer so as to build a community of users. In the business-to-business market this is often referred to as an "ecosystem" because it involves some tool, such as app development for a smartphone. Consequently, the community created is very much dependent on the business the company is in which is driven by its key component.

Although many businesses are branded, not many depend on their brand as much as the luxury goods industry. Brand marketing is about the customer experience: where and how the customer experiences the company's products. The experience is complete: It begins from how the customer experiences the brand before entering the retail location, continues with how they experience it within the location and then after they leave. Hollister, a clothing company, manages the look, feel and scent of their stores to provide their clients with a very specific experience somewhere between the country club and a club.

LVMH, a French luxury goods company, spends a great deal on sponsorship so that their brands are associated with luxury events like the America's Cup yacht racing. Remy Cointreau may sponsor the Bridgehampton Polo Challenge. Giorgio Armani and Prada recently got involved in the hotel business designing interiors.

Other marketers prefer the community engagement approach that combines event management with social media as a way of connecting a business with its target audience. Social media allows businesses to move away from the one-to-many/top-down forms of communication that traditional advertising imposes to a many-to-many/flat form of communication. Social media allows the business to communicate with its audience, the audience to respond, the audience members to engage amongst themselves and then brings into the discussion other individuals such as partners and vendors. I was told the story of a marketer who, while working for her client, tried to contact a large cruise line company by telephone and email, without receiving a response. Frustrated, she posted a message on Twitter and received a response in less than 24 hours! On top of that, the cruise line was interested in collaborating with her client. Increasingly, companies are having to relinquish control over the message in favor of participating actively with their community, so they keep a close eye on their social media accounts.

There are many ways of managing the risk of consumption, too many to go into here. Similarly, it is up to the business to come up with how to make that connection. I just mentioned a few basics to get you thinking about how to consider this challenge both regarding your own business as well as how the competition may behave. Whatever the choices made, if they don't help maintain the ROKC they will be a waste. So, it is important to stay focused.

Other Business Risks

Up to now we have explored risks that the attentive observer can identify but there are others that stem from areas of expertise and therefore are not readily identifiable. These other risks are financial, legal, cultural, political and so on. They are discussed separately because they may not be of interest to everyone, so you can skip this chapter if you want.

A few very basic financial risks are: credit terms, foreign exchange risk, interest rate risk, commodity prices, share valuations, market expectations, taxation, and so on.

Legal risks can include: bargaining power, differences in jurisdictional interpretation, labor relations, regulatory obligations, zoning ordinances, and warranty periods. There are many others.

Cultural risks are harder to identify and manage so we won't go into this area too much but suffice it to say that it is not because people in another part of the country or in another country entirely look like you and consume the same products as you that they will see the world through the same rose-tinted glasses as you do. Cultural differences can be very significant and should not be underestimated when expanding a business beyond the borders of where it is already established. Cultural sensitivity and adaptation may be required to gain acceptance not only of the business but of its products.

This book addresses the issue of leadership, so discussing risks requires addressing politics. Many people in business are also in politics or have political connections, so the two are often closely related. Taking into consideration political risks that may affect the business is a subject you don't want to miss. Who is in power, how that power is exercised and any other political issue may affect the business significantly. There are many direct and indirect risks like taxation and tax credits, expropriation, physical access to sites, rule of law, respect of contractual obligations, and many more.

Although not all these risks may affect the key component or the transformative process they may have an impact on the return itself, making them equally important. Each business will need to determine what risks affect the business and how, and the best strategy for managing each individual risk.

Talent Risks

As you may have already discerned, as important as it may be to have talented people working with the business on the transformative process, it is in risk management where truly talented people are required. If you remember that the transformative process where value creation occurs then you will quickly understand the company can accept small imperfections here. Likewise, if your recall that risk management predominantly destroys the value created by the transformative then you can imagine that any small imperfection here can have a potentially exponentially destructive impact on the ROKC. Consequently, the risk of having the most talented person in a risk management role is far more important for the business to succeed.

The first way to manage talent risk is to hire people with the assets that match the company's assets. In this case, a hire is comparable to an external professional who possesses their own key component. The only difference is the amount of time this person is required by the company, making it more economical to employ them directly. This one-person business partner helps the business succeed by using their own key component exclusively for the benefit of one client, an in-house client.

Accordingly, a company using Great Plains accounting software will seek to hire an "Accounting Expert in Great Plains." Similarly, a business using Magento e-Commerce Suite will not seek any old e-commerce specialist but one having "Experience with Magento." Or, a company using SAP will hire an expert in SAP, another using Six Sigma will want a black belt and so on and so forth. But it doesn't stop here, an apparel company will want a hire with industry or even sector experience: "Must have apparel industry experience." or "Must have 5 years in luxury women's footwear.", respectively.

As much as this approach tries to increase the chances that the hire knows how to use the company's assets when they walk in the door it, which reduces talent risk, it increases the risk of group think. The circulation of human resources within the same industry over time will blind everyone to systemic risks like those that brought the financial system in 2008. Back then, analysts priced financial products using a 40% recovery rate because it was considered the industry standard instead of questioning this one very important assumption which might have avoided the crash altogether, according to some industry experts. Bringing in a fresh set of eyes who contributes non-industry standard views can actually be more important for risk management than recruiters think.

In-house functions that cannot be manage risks with ease may be better done by outside specialist. These are companies who built their business on their key components and now sell them to help manage their client's risk. Traditionally, experts like doctors, lawyers, auditors, architects, psychologists, scholars fulfilled this role. Nowadays, there are whole battalions of local, national and international companies to whom a business can outsource their risks: warehousing, transportation, supply chain specialists, website hosting, cloud hosting, Saas, Iaas, App developers, e-commerce management services, order fulfillment, payment gateways, digital marketing agencies, engineering firms, security firms, shared services and so on.

Compared with the past when businesses did almost everything in-house, today companies are essentially flat. Or, as I like to say, an upside down banana peel; flat with a small rise in the middle. Today's modern businesses, especially the big ones, have become a swarm of businesses where each worker bee is specialized in its task. One business may buy the inputs for a product while another manages the supply chain that gets the inputs to where they need to be used, a shipping company gets the inputs there, and a contract manufacturer builds the product. Meanwhile, an IT company provides the software that allows everyone in the process to see what's going on and an accounting company posts the financial flows to the accounts of multiple legal entities above. While this is going on orders are being taken, advertising is being conceived of and produced, social media experts are tweeting, and so on. Each of these companies absorb a part of the risk traditionally held by the big company.

As we have argued throughout this book, the ROKC method focuses the business on its competitive advantage in order to maximize shareholder returns. But it can also maximizes stakeholder satisfaction. The decision to maintain a process and/or its risk management in-house, like the decision to externalize it, means that those talented people who work with the company on the ROKC will feel that they are providing real value. This brings real satisfaction to everyone.

Worksheet

Following the book, and adding to it where you require, use the SWOT analysis to identify the risks the business faces. Remember, we are only interested in risk management activities that affect ROKC.

For each risk determine the impact managing them has on the ROKC.

What assumptions are you making?

Examine each assumption used and revise every response up to this point until you can't go any further.

Leave your work alone for a week.

After a week review and refresh your work.

Leadership built on the ROKC

Leadership built on the ROKC

Everything proposed in this book cannot be achieved without someone assuming leadership for the process. Someone in the business needs to exercise the power - the ability to influence the outcome of decisions and events - to bring this management method about. Unlike the three blind men, each having only a fraction of the understanding of what an elephant looks like, the leader must be the one who has a vision of the whole: the whole elephant. The leader can then use this vision to influence what the elephant does in its environment.

Influencing the outcome of events inside a business is usually straightforward because it is organized for it. Outside it is more difficult for a leader to influence events, but if the whole organization is structured from the bottom up to move as a coherent whole this becomes possible.

Take the credit risk as an example. Most businesses extend credit to their customers by allowing them to pay some time in future after receiving the product, and this creates risk. The risk of not recovering the amount due is the credit risk. This risk can be managed in many ways and usually companies will use different techniques that involve buying products from other companies, like: Dun & Bradstreet reports, credit insurance, credit cards, and so on. All these risk mitigating activities remain centered on the business, which is fine but costly. Another way, a complementary way, is to talk with credit managers working in companies that serve the same client. Most customers are served by a whole host of vendors some which will be direct competitors but other will not be. For instance, if your company sells TVs chances are your client also sells vacuum cleaners or small electric appliances, so the two credit managers can talk about their common client without there being a conflict of interest. This course of action can reduce company expenditures (ex. stop buying credit insurance), be more effective by getting real market information in real time and help the company take a more sure footed path in the market.

Once in place, such actions that affect the company's short-term performance should be delegated to those who manage the day-to-day. Ideally, the business should be organized to run smoothly so that leadership can focus on the long-term objectives of the business.

The most basic way of ensuring the long-term is to keep constantly question the assumptions. As we have seen above, there are assumptions made at all levels and all those focus on the competitive advantage provided by the key component so leadership's task is to work with line managers on those assumptions without which the company could potentially turn into a dinosaur. This process provides leadership with the tools necessary to know when the key component's competitive advantage is waning seek a new one.

As the LVMH example illustrated, the key component probably started out as craftsmanship which was then taught to apprentices, next to engineers and so on until it reaches the brand. Too often, companies employ resources to manage the risks to an old key component instead of transitioning to a new one. A situation that can't be maintained for very long since it requires a disproportionate expenditure in risk management which reduces ROKC.

At least internally, the most significant advantage the ROKC method provides business leaders is the flexibility to change their strategic approach to the market as often as is required without jeopardizing the company's key component and the competitive advantage. I remember John Case, the CEO of Cisco, once saying something to effect that the company had changed strategies six times in year. He could do this because the key component was constant it was everything above that changed. Even in situations of catastrophic market failure, the company can still return money to shareholders if it preserved the key component by sell it.

Apple's iPod is a good example of the leadership built on the ROKC method. Apple created an integrated system that helps the music companies get a return on investment on their music libraries; this helps Apple get a return on investment on its iTunes system, Apple's contract manufacturers get a return on their factories by manufacturing the devices and selling them to Apple and the end-user to get a return on investment through the hours of pleasure they get from using their devices.

It is important to note that at the center of all this is the iTunes store, the key component. Almost everything Apple did after developing the iTunes store was to get return on it. If we look at the company's history we may be able to see this more clearly.

January 2001 - launch of iTunes
May 2001 - first retail store
October 2001 - first iPod launched
October 2003 - iTunes made available for Windows
June 2005 - adopted Intel processors
October 2005 - TV shows added to iTunes
September 2006 - Movies added to iTunes
January 2007 - company drops "computers" from its name
May 2007 - adds iTunes U for educational content
June 2007 - launched iPhone
July 2008 - App store is launched

April 2010 - launched iPad and added books to iTunes
Fall 2013 - radio added to iTunes

Since the turn of the century, Apple has progressively and aggressively redefined itself as a distributor of content, moving all manner of digital products through its iTunes store. The focus and drive to achieve this strategic change are remarkable. Not every business can do this but I do hold Apple up as an example of a remarkably focused company.

This means that leaders who build on the ROKC also show integrity and are credible in the eyes of shareholders and stakeholders. Both very highly valued attributes for a leader.

Worksheet

Is company leadership committed to the ROKC method?

Business Planning

The best way of applying the ROKC method in your business is to start with the business planning process and then rolling out the management system throughout the business. For clarity, the roll out involves aligning the business's structure and functions around the key component's competitive advantage.

Let me preface this chapter by saying I am a big fan of the business plan. They are great for capturing all the strategic information about a business, for creating consensus around the underlying assumptions and are useful for communicating the company's strategic vision inside the business and to key partners outside.

The traditional business plan is designed to take the reader from the general to the specific. It starts with the overall market, segments it by competitor, looks at what the competition is doing before using the SWOT analysis to transition to the internal workings of the company. Once inside the company all the whys and wherefores are presented explaining what the company will do to achieve that top-line growth and the resources necessary for it. Lastly, a nice set of financial statements will present how this translates into dollars and cents, or some other currency.

The major drawback is human error. Most people don't write business plans properly because they don't always ask the questions that get to the very foundations of the business. Usually, business plan writers just start in the middle and work their way out until they have fulfilled the requirements, but never look at the assumptions or the assumptions of the assumptions.

A business plan is structured like a lawyer's argument in a big trial. An argument has assumptions and premises underpinning it and exists in a clearly defined space. Like with an argument, a business plan review should never focus on the argument itself but on the assumptions and premises. If you don't do this the review becomes a mathematical exercise that is of no interest and the marketplace will quickly let you know how unrealistic you may have been.

All the important issues we addressed in this book are often not asked. The most basic question that investigates why the business exists is not asked: What is the key component? All the questions about the validity of the business's key component are not asked: the competitive advantage. No real questions are asked about the transformative process that allows the company to maximize its ROKC. More importantly, the company will compare itself with the competition potentially falling into a group think appreciation of performance.

When I was a child we would go on car trips and my father would play a really annoying game with us: The Why Game. It consisted of him asking us "why" to whatever we answered. He might start with "Why is the sky blue?" Then my brother, sister or I would give a response and he would ask us why to whatever the response was. I hated this game because it quickly became frustrating. You could never win. Nonetheless, this is a great way to prepare a business plan because you question everything.

I was recently introduced to a prospective client who for two hours painstakingly tried to explain his business to me without ever convincing me of its validity. In fact, he was a potential client because his business didn't work any more and he didn't know why. I listened and asked questions during our time together, thanked him for his hospitality and agreed to take him on as a client. I already knew what his problem was. He was unable to identify his business's key component and the competitive advantage it gave him. As a result he couldn't organize the business properly. Lucky for me, from our talk, I already had an idea what his key component was so I could get my own ROKC!

The ROKC method emphasizes the importance of identifying the key component and the competitive advantage it gives the business. It keeps a clean distinction between the transformative process and all the risk management activities that may have an impact on the business model affecting the ROKC. This conceptual framework obliges the writer of the business plan to question everything. So the business plan should have the same organization as the book.

1. Executive Summary
2. The Key Component
3. Transformative Process
    3.1. Productive Process
    3.2. Consumption Process
4. Business Model & Mission Statement
5. Risk Management
    5.1. Competitive Advantage Risks
    5.2. Productive Process Risks
    5.3. Consumption Risks
    5.4. Other Risks
    5.5. Talent Risks
    5.6. Leadership Risks
    5.7. Cost of Capital & Return on Investment
6. Annex
    6.1. Financials
    6.2. Presentation

By following the book you can think about your business in a strategic way and use that clarity to improve the efficacy of your decision-making, which should result in a maximum ROKC for all stakeholders.

This may sound like overkill, but after having done all that we have done together it is not a good idea to turn back. What I want to suggest is a totally different approach to financial statement preparation that focuses on the structure we have developed here. Since each company presents their accounts differently, I don't want to cause the accountants to have a heart attack; keep the system you have in place. But split the business up into its component parts so you can maintain the clarity developed from applying the ROKC method. Using a spreadsheet make a financial statement for the key component and its risks, the productive process and its risks, the consumptive process and its risks, cost of capital and its risks, talent and leadership and their risks before summarize everything into a total company view. This way you can see how each decision affects company performance.

You may even want to take the analysis a bit further by treating each area like an activity, a sort of Activity Based Costing approach, for the financial readers, and use the profit generated by the business model to pay for the risk management activities. This has the added benefit of indicating whether this activity should be made or bought. In some cases, it may be better to externalize the activity. While in other cases, your risk management activity may be so much better than the competition that you spin it off as a separate business that can service other clients thus getting even more value.

If your business has different product lines and/or divisions then by all means split those too. By doing this you can derive the greatest benefit this framework offers. Every change to how the business transforms or sells a product will trickle down to the cash generated.

Lastly, you can calculate the return on invested capital and see how every tweak affects the end result.

Once you have done your first business plan, you can start to organize your business around the ROKC method and start to really see the benefits in terms of maximizing shareholder returns and stakeholder satisfaction.

Worksheet

Based on your last iteration write an actionable plan over a maximum period of 3 to 5 years.

Using the action plan, create a cash basis financial projection for the business.

Based on the results, revise everything up to this point until satisfied.

Develop a financing structure for the business using capital and debt. Make assumptions about the cost of capital.

Revise the financial projection for interest expense and income/corporate taxes.

Revise the financing structure until satisfied.

The Cost of Capital & ROI

Ideally, a product will find its own place in the market and generate its own profits for reinvestment without there being an initial cash investment. This is, however, very unlikely. Some form of initial investment is usually required. It is this initial and possibly subsequent outlay of cash that interests us.

Some entrepreneurs invest their own money before asking for capital from the 4Fs (Friends, Family, Faithful, and Fools). Others opt for crowdfunding as a means to acquire initial capital. After this phase, Angel money might be sought, and if all goes well, Venture Capital then Private Equity before an IPO. Likewise, the business may seek loans to raise cash.

What business's often fail to grasp is this money comes with a price, the cost of capital. Investors want the business to return the capital invested and they want a return for the use of their money, or the ROI, Return on Investment.

In calculating the ROI there are four basic components to consider:

1. Amount invested - a lump sum or paid out over time.
2. Future cash flows - cash generated and consumed during a period of time.

3. The investment horizon - time.
4. Market expectations

Time is a very important business concept, often underestimated outside the Anglo-Saxon world, because the ROI can be higher or lower depending on time. This is where market expectations come into play.

The market may expect a certain ROI on capital invested for one month and another if the capital is used for many years. Look in any newspaper at the rates on government bonds and you will see different yields at 1, 3, 6 months and 1, 5, 10, 30 years. An investor's decision to invest in the asset which is your company will be influenced by alternative investments like government and corporate bonds, money market accounts, CDs, and any number of other financial instruments available in the market as well as other companies. Keep in mind the ROI is only calculated in cash.

Think of it this way: The business borrows $100 from the bank at 5% per year; and invests $50 in its key component and uses the rest in the transformative process. The price at which the product is sold must generate enough money to return the $100 to the bank plus whatever interest the bank gets for lending the company the money. The interest is calculated as some fraction of time multiplied by the 5% p.a. interest rate.

So far so good for bank who supported the company but not for the shareholders? Did they get paid? No. So, the profit the business generates needs to pay them too. But an investor can only calculate their ROI when the company gives them money. If the company is large, then maybe there is a dividend policy which returns money to shareholders every quarter or year. Or, if the company stock is traded on an exchange shares can be bought and sold thus providing a capital gain. A small company will not want to issue dividends because cash is necessary to the company's survival.

A small company will want to have a liquidity event during which investors can sell their shares to a new investor to make their ROI. In this case, the profit the business makes needs to be reinvested to make the shares more valuable allowing investors to sell their shares when the next round of financing is achieved. The higher the number of rounds of financing the opportunities there are for investors to get a return until the ultimate "exit" is accomplished from the sale of the company to either a private company or to the public through an IPO.

The cost of capital is the price the business must pay for using an investor's capital. The cost will vary according to the ROI market conditions dictate for each type of financing the business has: equity, preferred shares, debt, and so on.

How much the ROI is depends on market conditions. As we saw above there are many financial instruments in the market and where a business is within that spectrum is specific to the characteristics of the business itself.

Capital is returned to investors from profit and must leave enough cash in the business to ensure its future.

Worksheet

Calculate the return on invested capital.

Worksheet

Formalize the business plan.

Create a presentation and deck to share with stakeholders.

Worksheet

On separate paper, answer as many of the following questions as you can and place them in a binder. Or, use your computer. Refer back to your previous answers as you work through the successive ones and update as necessary.

1. What is your business's key component? The asset that gives your business a competitive advantage in its market.
2. What is the competitive advantage the key component provides your business in the market(s) within which it operates?
3. Describe the process by which the business transforms the key component into a product.
4. How do customers perceive the benefits and value of the product?
5. How does the business create a win-win situation with its customers?
6. Describe your business model.
7. Write your company's mission statement.
8. How much ROKC does the business model create?
9. Following the book, and adding to it where you require, use the SWOT analysis to identify the risks the business faces. **Remember, we are only interested in risk management activities that affect ROKC.**
10. For each risk determine the impact managing them has on the ROKC.

11. What assumptions are you making?
12. Examine each assumption used and revise every response up to this point until you can't go any further.
13. Leave your work alone for a week.
14. After a week review and refresh your work.
15. Is company leadership committed to the ROKC method?
16. Based on your last iteration write an actionable plan over a maximum period of 3 to 5 years.
17. Using the action plan, create a cash basis financial projection for the business.
18. Based on the results, revise everything up to this point until satisfied.
19. Develop a financing structure for the business using capital and debt. Make assumptions about the cost of capital.
20. Revise the financial projection for interest expense and income/corporate taxes.
21. Revise the financing structure until satisfied.
22. Calculate the return on invested capital.
23. Formalize the above into a business plan.
24. Create a presentation and deck to share with stakeholders.

If you want to be accompanied in this process, please contact us to schedule an appointment.

www.returnonkeyinvestment.com
contact@returnonkeyinvestment.com

Printed in Great Britain
by Amazon